Climbing MT. self

KENRIC WILLIAMS

A'LURE PUBLISHING, LLC

Climbing MT. self

Copyright © 2024 by Kenric Williams

All rights reserved. This book or any portion thereof may not be reproduced or used without the publisher and author's express written permission, except for brief quotations in critical articles or short reviews.

For more information, contact:
alurepublishing.net
alurepublishingllc@gmail.com
T: 919-391-8502
ISBN: 979-8-9902920-3-1 (Paperback)
Library of Congress Control Number: 2024916661
Publication Date: October 2, 2024
First Edition: October 2024

Climbing MT. self

I want to dedicate this book to family, friends, and my crown jewels, Chrissy and Christopher.

Also, to my amazing parenting partner and the best woman I've had the blessing to meet, Schundra D. Hubbard.

To my amazing grandchildren, Kamari, Kenndi, KJ, Demi, and CJ.

CONTENTS

CHAPTER 1 9
RAISED IN QUICKSAND 9
CHAPTER 2 18
SINKING DEEPER 18
CHAPTER 3 23
GRABBING THE ROPE 23
CHAPTER 4 30
PULLING MYSELF UP 30
CHAPTER 5 36
CLEARING THE RUBBLE 36
CHAPTER 6 41
LAYING A NEW FOUNDATION 41
CHAPTER 7 47
BECOMING A BUILDER 47

CHAPTER 8 52

EMBRACING TRUE STRENGTH 52

CHAPTER 9 57

TRUSTING THE UNSEEN 57

CHAPTER 10 62

LIVING IN THE LIGHT 62

CHAPTER 1

RAISED IN QUICKSAND

I was seven years old, lying awake late at night alone, listening to them fight intensely for hours in the next room. Yell. Smack. Scream. Then, silence. Moments of silence offered no reassurance as I theorized worst-case scenarios of what would happen next. Is it over? It felt like a real-life scary movie—the kind I'd watch with my cousins on weekends.

Life was agonizingly unpredictable when my mother's abusive boyfriend came into our lives. His presence contributed to planting the seeds of self-rejection and fear that would later take root.

My mother was my world for the first nine years of my life. She was a single mother just trying to keep her head above water. She didn't have the insight to make better choices in her younger years. Born into a strict family void of an understanding and attentive environment, she repeated certain patterns and did her best during her younger years. My mom and I initially tried to survive without any life skills or a true sense of awareness.

Uncertainty was a constant in my life as a child. There were times when my mother would come into my room in the middle of the night, clutching me to her chest as her hot tears hit my skin to awaken me. The wetness burned my soul. I wouldn't move or speak in the darkness while I felt her trembling. I was paralyzed and felt helpless, and that left an indelible mark on me.

As a child, I felt I should do something to help the person I loved the most. What if I, her son, could've helped her? I internalized the blame and never spoke of it. I felt responsible—an illogical accountability that small children often internalize. Worrying became a constant activity, and the fear began building, planting seeds of fear and doubt. It was a heavy burden for a child to bear, and it marked me. It felt like I was in quicksand. The self-negating, shame, and guilt began. I was small and shy, and I began to retreat further inward. This was when I began to hide in plain sight, as I will explain later.

Seeds of doubt are often planted when least expected. When you're a child, these seeds are inadvertently planted in difficult moments and unintentionally watered. Self-doubt, self-neglect, and shame spring from them, and these hindrances are nourished in certain environments.

RAISED IN QUICKSAND

The most searing memory of terror was worrying whether or not my mother would make it back from work one day. With so many instances of screaming on the way home, my young mind feared a fatal crash. Introverted and sensitive, with a fierce attachment to my mother, this was my greatest fear. Not only did her boyfriend not try to take the place of my absent father, but he also hijacked any chance of feeling safe; it rocked me to the core. Sure, he was a monster in every sense of the word, but I had never known what a real man looked like. All of the ones I knew were either absent or always putting me down. What a real man looks like would elude me until I was 32 years old.

When we moved in with my mom's sister, discipline turned into a cruel punishment when she discovered my tendency to wet the bed. However, she inadvertently taught me to react quickly and gain awareness of my surroundings. To avoid whippings with the coat hanger, I would change my urine-soaked bed sheets faster than a NASCAR tire changer, so no one would see. The physical pain and shame from the beatings would be as intense as my ability to think on my feet. While it kept me on my toes, it never helped my identity or self-esteem. From this, self-rejection and negative thinking would grow. Her other sisters gossiped behind her back, trying to belittle us.

When my little brother, Darius, finally came along, I was hopeful things would improve. After all, the abuser would now have a flesh-and-blood son to focus on, which I hoped would shift his attention and even inspire him to change. Small for my age and shy, I was excited to have a sibling smaller than me and another boy with whom I could share the burden of a tumultuous life. We could have moments of camaraderie and laughter. I no longer had to face the scary movies with cousins alone, and I was no longer the only child returning to an empty house filled with the ghosts of my fears. But at the end of the day, my brother was the abuser's son. He had a father; I did not.

As time passed, the weight of my responsibilities as an older brother began to settle on my shoulders. Suddenly, I wasn't just responsible for navigating my fears and insecurities; I had to protect and care for my brother, too. Resentment started to simmer beneath the surface, mingling with the ever-present sense of inadequacy. I loved my brother deeply, but a part of me longed for the days when I only had myself to worry about.

With our home life unstable and without change in our abuser's behavior, we found ourselves moving in with my mom's sisters. I thought this would be a chance for a fresh start, a way out of the abuse and quicksand that threatened to consume us. But instead, I was met with judgment and gossip. They would whisper behind my mother's back, criticizing her every move as she tried desperately to keep our family afloat. I could see the toll it took on her—the way she would crumble under the weight of their words, her spirit slowly eroding with each passing day.

Yet she kept pushing forward, doing everything in her power to give us a better life and to shield us from the harsh realities of the world. She took a job for three dollars an hour. She tried everything in her power to give us what we needed. Watching her struggle and seeing the sacrifices she made, my heart ached for her.

School gradually became a battleground. There was a spotlight on my insecurities for all to see. In fourth grade, my uncle took it upon himself to cut my hair. As he worked, he cracked jokes at my expense, filling the room with laughter to my horror.

"There ain't no help in this head," he declared, his words cutting more profoundly than any blade.

The embarrassment hit me heavily, as I was the dark-skinned one, particularly sensitive and shy. My mom's family were the good-looking ones, I thought. When he was finished, I was left with a glaring bald spot that was impossible to hide. I had to wear a hat to school. My mom had to beg the teacher to let me keep it on, and my cheeks would burn with embarrassment every time I had to explain why. It was just another reminder of how different I was and how I needed to fit in.

I constantly compared my life to everyone else's, particularly my light-skinned cousin. He was the "pretty boy" all the girls loved, with his good hair and easy charm. Next to him, I felt like the ugly duckling, the dark-skinned misfit who would never measure up. Retreating further into myself, I hid my true feelings behind a mask of jokes and bravado, desperate to find some way to be accepted and to feel like I belonged. Of course, at the time, I was consumed with everybody looking at Michael Jackson and Prince, and I felt like I didn't stand a chance.

However, there were some bright spots. There were times when I felt connected, and my perspective shifted. That was the stuff I wanted to hang on to. My eighth-grade teacher, Mr. Jones, had a tremendous influence on me. I made friends in the eighth grade that I still have to this day, but the shift in perception was short-lived.

School became a daily reminder of everything I lacked, a constant comparison game that I could never win. I watched my classmates show off their new clothes and gadgets, things I could only ever dream of having. Each day, I felt the gulf between us growing wider, my own sense of inadequacy consuming me, eating away at my already fragile self-esteem. I was obsessed with having lots of fancy things—things I didn't have. Trying to compensate, I became a jack of all trades, dabbling in a little bit of everything in a desperate attempt to find my place, to carve out some small corner of the world where I could feel like I belonged. But no matter what I did, I felt like a master of none, always falling short, always wanting more than I had.

Entering my teenage years, the unresolved pre-teenage traumas began to take their toll, manifesting in ways I couldn't even begin to understand. Shame, guilt, and a deep sense of inferiority became my constant companions, a twisted soundtrack playing on repeat in my mind. I found myself constantly comparing myself to everyone else, convinced that I was fundamentally broken in some way, that I would never be good enough, and that I would never measure up to the impossible standards I set for myself. Little did I know that it was my perspective that was flawed.

To cope, I retreated behind a façade of humor and bravado, using jokes and sports as a way to feel some semblance of control and pretend that I was okay even as I was falling apart inside. I started smoking weed. But even that wasn't enough to quiet the voices in my head telling me I would never be good enough. It felt like I would never escape the quicksand that threatened to swallow me whole.

In desperation, I reached out to my well-off grandfather, pouring my heart out in a letter asking for money to buy new school clothes. For weeks, I waited, checking the mail every day with a glimmer of hope in my heart, praying that he would come through for me and that he would be the one to pull me out of the quicksand. But a response never came. It wasn't until years later, as he lay on his deathbed, that he finally acknowledged my plea. With tears in his eyes, he apologized for not sending the money when I needed it most and for not being there when I needed him. But by then, it was too late. My heart was hardened, and I had already turned to the streets, convinced hustling was the only way to get what I thought I needed.

Looking back, I can see how the emotional quicksand of my childhood contributed to my faulty mindset. I was set up to hide behind many masks just to survive. My fears, resentments, and insecurities became the lens through which I viewed the world, coloring every interaction and decision I made. I had no idea at the time, but this way of operating would follow me well into adulthood, leading me down a path of self-destruction and pain, a path that would take me to the very brink of oblivion before I found my way back to solid ground.

I thought I had finally found a way to escape the quicksand that had held me captive for so long. I thought I was ready to leave my past behind to forge a new path for myself. Little did I know, I was about to sink even deeper into the abyss and lose myself in a world of addiction and irresponsibility that would nearly destroy me. The road ahead was fraught with danger, heartbreak, and despair, but it was a road I had to travel to find my way back to myself and to the person I was meant to be. Ultimately, the only way out was through a lesson I would learn through years of trial and error, countless mistakes, and moments of grace through the love and support of those who refused to give up on me, even when I had given up on myself. But that is a story for another chapter—a story of sinking deeper before finally learning to swim.

CHAPTER 2

SINKING DEEPER

The quicksand of my addiction had been slowly pulling me under for years, and by my late teens, I was floundering and sinking deeper with each passing day. Every decision I made seemed to drag me further down, and I felt powerless to stop it.

I barely managed to graduate high school, scraping by with the bare minimum effort. I dreamed of becoming an electrician, but when I failed the apprenticeship math test, I simply shrugged and walked away.

"Fuck it," I muttered under my breath, unwilling to face the rejection and put in the work to try again. It was one of many moments where I let myself sink deeper into the mire of my own making.

Desperate for some semblance of stability, I took a job at a grocery store. But even there, my ego and chip-on-my-shoulder street hustle mentality made me think I could do it all. I thought I was an invincible multitasker, capable of juggling work, partying, and dealing drugs on the side. I wasn't present at the job, and my mind was always scheming about how to make a quick buck. I was so good at sizing people up and figuring out what I could get from them that I began to sell cocaine to my own boss, supplying him with eight balls three times a week.

I was just pissing away the money as fast as I was making it. I threw wild parties in the building where I worked, renting out apartments and trashing them with reckless abandon. One particularly memorable bash was for my best friend's brother's high school graduation. We threw a massive rooftop party that spiraled out of control, leaving the apartment in shambles and the police at the door.

The next morning, my boss called me into his office, detailing the astronomical damages. But unbeknownst to him, I had all the money in my pocket—nearly $3,000. Without batting an eye, but with bravado, I paid the damages on the spot. He was impressed, and he let me keep my job. Little did he know, however, I was just trying to seem cool while covering my own ass.

For years, I faked having it together at work, hiding my double life behind a façade of responsibility. But I was just deflecting in order to neglect everything that truly mattered. I wasn't taking care of my responsibilities at home; I was bouncing between women, and I was sinking deeper into the soulless abyss of addiction.

When my daughter Chrissy was born during my sophomore year of high school, I was secretly elated and terrified, which paralyzed me. I was haunted every minute, hour, and day, as the responsibility of having a child was overwhelming. How could I be a father to someone when I was still a child myself? The way I dealt with that was to barely acknowledge her existence. I was too wrapped up in my own selfish pursuits to be a father to her, and I was oblivious to the magnitude of the repercussions of my actions.

It wasn't until Christopher was born on December 29, 1994, and I was in my 20s that I began to realize any semblance of responsibility. As I looked into his intense eyes, a perfect mirror of my own, I was stopped dead in my tracks. How could I possibly model being a good man for this child when I was struggling so much just to exist in this world? His gaze felt like a tacit challenge, and it scared me to death.

But even that moment of clarity wasn't enough to pull me out of the quicksand. I continued to spiral, my ego convincing me that I could hustle full-time and leave my job behind. It was a disastrous decision that only accelerated my descent into harder drugs like cocaine and heroin.

My self-destructive behavior finally reached a breaking point when my mother kicked me out of the house at age 17. She had found cocaine paraphernalia and a .22 pistol in my room, and she had reached her limit. In a fit of rage, I retaliated, screaming and cursing at her until she told me to get out. I had the audacity to scream and curse at my own mother. I was 17 years old, and I never went back to live in that house again.

From that moment on, my ego was in full force. I fully committed to choosing the streets over my relationship with my family. I severed my last lifeline, and the quicksand began to spread and thrive, consuming every aspect of my life.

I found myself in and out of jail, each time thinking that this would be the wake-up call I needed to change. But inevitably, as soon as I was released, I would fall right back into the predictable cycle due to the clutches of addiction. The craving for heroin was so strong that I would feel it deep in my bones just from seeing the city skyline, even after years of being locked up. It was a sickness that had taken hold of my body and my mind, and I felt powerless to stop it.

The emotional quicksand of my addiction soon turned into literal homelessness. I slept in abandoned cars, huddled in warming centers, and begged God to help me change my ways. I would promise Him anything, swearing that if He just got me out of this hell, I would turn my life around. But time and time again, I found myself pulled back into the cycle of addiction, unable to escape its grasp.

My lowest point came on one of the coldest nights in Chicago's history. Desperate for warmth, I went to my mother's house and begged her to let me stand in her hallway just to escape the biting cold. But she didn't even open the door. Instead, she closed the curtain without a word, leaving me to fend for myself in the frigid darkness.

But even in that moment of utter despair, I couldn't find it in myself to be angry with her. Deep down, I knew I had brought this upon myself. These were my decisions and my choices alone. Her rejection only fueled my subconscious determination to change, to claw my way out of the quicksand and become the man I knew I could be.

The road ahead would be long and arduous, but somewhere in the depths of my being, a tiny spark of hope began to flicker. If I could just find something to grab onto—some lifeline to pull me out of this mess—maybe I stood a chance. Maybe, just maybe, there was a way out of the darkness and into the light.

That spark of hope would prove to be the turning point in my journey—the first glimmer of a rope that would eventually lead me out of the quicksand and onto solid ground. But the climb would be treacherous, and I would need every ounce of strength and determination to see it through.

The path to redemption was waiting, but first, I had to find the courage to reach out and grab it.

CHAPTER 3

GRABBING THE ROPE

October 1st, 2003, is a date that will forever be etched in my memory. It was both my rock bottom and my salvation. Homeless, dope-sick, and consumed by desperation, I found myself trapped in a vicious cycle of addiction and going nowhere fast. My daily ritual consisted of copping drugs, grabbing a newspaper, and walking to the police station, determined to turn myself in on an outstanding warrant. Yet, each time I approached the station, I would chicken out. My courage would wither, and I would lose my resolve at the last minute every time.

The addiction pulled me deeper into the quicksand than ever before. I was sleeping on the streets, eating nothing, and not even bothering to bathe. Basic hygiene was the last thing on my mind, and that was how I presented myself to the world. I felt invisible. My clothes stuck to my body like a second skin, the only things willing to be close to me. But on that fateful day in October, something inside shifted and made me say to myself, "I'm turning myself in today."

Before reaching the police station, I encountered a group of guys who were having a "pass out," a term used when drug dealers give free samples to addicts. It was a common occurrence. As I waited in line for one last fix, the police suddenly appeared out of nowhere, putting everyone on the ground. Chaos ensued as I watched my friends being chased and arrested—another common occurrence—and something inside me clicked into the present moment. I snapped out of listening to the chaotic dog whistle that elicited a reactionary response. I didn't need the chaos. Neither did I need to follow the pack. Somehow, that was the beginning of me paying attention to my individual will. I was also simply too tired to run. At that moment, I knew I needed to move toward the light and get some kind of help.

I flagged down an officer and confessed, "Hey man, I got a warrant." The officer, taken aback, asked what the warrant was for.

"Aggravated robbery," I replied, my voice trembling. His eyes widened as he ran my name through the system, confirming the outstanding warrant. What happened next was a testament to the officer's compassion and my own desperation.

Without hesitation, I opened the door to the police car and climbed in, ready to face the consequences of my actions. The officer, in a surprising display of humanity, didn't even bother to handcuff me. As we drove away, I knew that I was headed toward the unknown and that my dance with the demons was moving farther away.

October 2nd, 2003, marks my sobriety date, but the irony is that I actually used drugs on October 1st. The man I shared a cell with had managed to sneak in some contraband, and in a moment of weakness, I succumbed to temptation one last time. But from that day forward, I vowed to leave all mind-altering substances behind. I was done.

Facing five more years in prison, I had nothing left to lose. I didn't know how to change, but I prayed fervently to be sent somewhere with real help this time. It was a moment of surrender, a "fuck it" moment where I finally acknowledged that I couldn't do it alone.

What happened next can only be described as divine intervention. As I went through the intake process at Stateville Penitentiary, a compassionate officer saw the desperation in my eyes.

She looked at me and asked, "Young man, if I get you some help, will you take it?"

Without hesitation, I replied, "Ma'am, I will do anything I must do. I'm tired."

It was a major turning point. She told me about a new drug treatment program at Sheridan Correctional Center, where the entire facility was dedicated to rehabilitation. The program, run by the Gateway Foundation, offered a glimmer of hope in the darkness that had consumed my life. When she asked if I would take the help if she could get me in, I answered with a resounding, "Absolutely."

That officer, whose name I never learned, became my guardian angel. She didn't talk to anyone else or go through the usual bureaucratic channels. Instead, she single-handedly secured my placement in the Sheridan program, and with that, my journey of recovery began.

For two and a half years, I immersed myself in the program, attending eight hours of intense group therapy, addiction education, and counseling every day. At first, I approached it with the mindset of an inmate, just going through the motions. I was skeptical and unwilling. But the counselors saw through my façade and refused to let me hide behind my bullshit. They were patient, and their confrontations were delivered with a blend of toughness and love. This forced me to look at and acknowledge the reality of my situation.

It was in one of those groups that something clicked. I sat through session after session, listening to the counselors speak without really listening. There was a wall that couldn't be penetrated, and I just sat there like a lox. But after months of hearing them pour their hearts out into their work, gradually, their words started to make sense.

They were in recovery themselves, and one day, I felt their wisdom, and it melted me. They cared for the people they were trying to help, and they had the tools to back it up. They weren't just dealing on a surface level. They were walking the talk. I could finally feel it and let the walls start to come down. For the first time in my life, I allowed myself to consider the possibility of change.

During my time at Sheridan, I met a man who would become my first true mentor. I was 32 years old at the time. Steve Harmon, the chief electrician at the facility, took me under his wing and treated me like a son. He taught me the intricacies of wiring and electricity, but more importantly, he showed me what it meant to be a man of integrity.

Steve would bring food from home, knowingly breaking the rules to provide me with a taste of the outside world. He would also quell my hunger for connection. He would sit with me while sharing stories about his family and imparting wisdom that would stay with me for a lifetime. Through his actions and words, he demonstrated the value of hard work, responsibility, and compassion. This was a healing relationship with someone who modeled the behavior of a true man.

Under Steve's guidance, I thrived in the program. I turned in all my assignments, became a leader among my peers, and was given the privilege of working alongside Steve on the facility's electrical system. He saw potential in me that I had never recognized in myself, and his unwavering belief in my ability to change was a catalyst for my transformation.

The combination of Steve's paternal love and the intensive program finally penetrated the walls I had built around my heart and mind. I started grabbing every rope thrown my way, taking the lifelines offered to me and using them to pull myself out of the abyss of addiction.

October 2nd, 2003, became my true starting point. It was the day I grabbed the rope, took charge of my life, and embarked on the journey of recovery. I realized that God had been working through people like Steve and the compassionate intake officer to show me a way out. All I needed was the desperate willingness to take it, even if I didn't feel worthy or even understand what true recovery meant.

Looking back, I can see that grabbing that rope saved my life. It was the first step in a long and challenging climb, but it was a step I had to take. With each passing day, I pulled myself a little bit further out of the quicksand, slowly but surely making my way towards the light.

GRABBING THE ROPE

As I reflect on that pivotal moment in my life, I am filled with gratitude for the people who saw something in me worth saving. Their compassion, combined with my own desperation, set in motion a chain of events that would forever alter the course of my existence.

Grabbing the rope was just the beginning. The real work lay ahead, and I knew that I would have to summon every ounce of strength and determination to keep pulling myself up, one day at a time. The journey of recovery had only just begun, and I was ready to face the challenges that lay ahead. I was armed with a newfound sense of purpose and the unwavering support of those who believed in me.

CHAPTER 4

PULLING MYSELF UP

The real work of recovery began after I achieved sobriety. Putting down the drinks and drugs was only the first step in a long journey of healing and rebuilding. To truly transform my life, I had to retrain my thinking, connect with others who had walked this path before me, and reconstruct my existence brick by brick. The only way out of the rubble was to pull myself up by the bootstraps and do the hard work of change.

In 2006, after completing two and a half years of intensive prison treatment, I moved into a recovery house called *It's About Change.* The CEO of the program, a man named Anthony, took me under his wing and became my AA sponsor. I met Anthony when I was done working with Steve. He poured healing into my life in a way I had never experienced before.

I was going up to my cell to try to sneak in a nap before dinner.

My counselor said, "Come here, Williams."

PULLING MYSELF UP

I came down, and she wanted me to talk with Anthony Dillard, the guy who owned the recovery home that I was about to be paroled to. I didn't know where I was going, but when he told me he only had one recovery home and wanted me there, I felt his sincerity and knew this was my place. I made the decision then and there to go with him while I was still in jail. After I was released, I went straight to the recovery home.

Anthony taught me an invaluable lesson: always find someone in the program you aspire to be like—a person of integrity who models the principles of recovery in their daily life. I began emulating him, soaking up his wisdom and guidance. He saw potential in me and gave me responsibility as house manager, taking me to recovery conferences, jail talks, and events. For the first time in my life, I was walking into prison through the front door by choice, offering hope to those still trapped in the cycle of addiction.

Through his mentorship, Anthony laid the foundation for my service and helped me adjust to the outside world. But after a decade of working with him, I realized I needed more. I was going through the motions but not really working the steps. For at least ten years, I was just regular. I worked every day, paid my bills, and was kind to people. I helped others, trying to get acclimated back into society, but inside, I still felt like a dirtbag. I was just doing everything to get it done without plugging into anything spiritual. I was still living just for myself.

Desperate for true healing, I sought out an AA legend named Mahat, who became my next sponsor. He was a 12-step fundamentalist and "Big Book thumper" who took me through the harder, deeper work of rigorous honesty and change. Mahat introduced me to the door, giving me the framework for the 12-step process for real, not just for show. He put me in a situation where I had to confront the fact that if I wasn't doing the work, I wasn't really in the program.

I couldn't just say, "Hey, I'm Ken; I'm an alcoholic," and call it a day. I had to dive into the steps and understand the spiritual component connected to each one. Without that, I was just a dressed-up garbage can.

Mahat force-fed me the Big Book, line by line, word by word, not moving on until he was sure every person in the room grasped the concepts. At this point, it was all rote for me. I understood it, but it wasn't in my bones. He taught me that the book wasn't just meant to be read but studied, internalized, and applied.

During his Wednesday night meetings, he would have a "dictionary person" on hand to look up any words we didn't understand. The meeting would screech to a halt until everyone was on the same page. He was relentless. Mahat was a master at breaking down the medical, mental, and spiritual components of addiction. He showed me that I would remain a stranger to myself until I faced the fool in the mirror. The jokester kid in me disappeared, and a man took his place.

Under Mahat's guidance, I did a searching and fearless moral inventory, the fourth step in the program. He helped me see that I was selfish, self-seeking, inconsiderate, and filled with resentment and fear. The truth was painful, but it began to set me free. Mahat wouldn't let me off the hook or half-ass the steps. He insisted that I go all the way through to step twelve if I wanted lasting change. He taught me to get over myself and let God into my life.

When Mahat fell ill, I knew I needed a new sponsor to keep pulling me up. I asked Rob, another no-nonsense guru, to take me on. He reminded me never to get complacent and that recovery requires constant seeking.

In May of 2017, Rob called me and asked, "Hey, what are you gonna do?"

I heard the tone in his voice. He had been telling me for a while that I needed to raise the bar, and I thought I was doing good just by meeting with him. But when he called me out, I knew I was bullshitting myself. I wasn't digging as deep as I could. At that moment, I made the decision to go all in. From that day forward, I haven't taken my foot off the accelerator.

Rob challenged my ego and made me take a daily inventory of my actions and motives. He taught me to pause and pray before every interaction so I could show up with the right heart. I learned to pick up the phone and call him every day; isolation is not an option.

As he says, "We stay connected to stay protected."

To maintain my sobriety, I had to build my life around prayer, meetings, and fellowship. As I worked the steps and rebuilt my life, I also had to repair the relationships I had shattered in my addiction. It took years to regain the trust of my kids, Chrissy and Christopher, their mother, and my own mom. Apologies weren't enough; I had to pull myself up and show them through my consistently changed actions that I was becoming a new man. I started showing up for them in ways I never had before, being present and accountable. It's something that doesn't happen overnight.

Brick by brick, I pulled myself out of the rubble of my past and reconstructed my life through the program. I had to put in the hard work, face ugly truths about myself, make amends, and humble myself to God's will. There are no shortcuts in recovery; there is no easy way out. But as I cleared away the wreckage and built a new foundation, I discovered a strength and resilience I never knew I had. The process of pulling myself up taught me that I am capable of overcoming any obstacle, one day at a time.

With a firm foundation beneath me, I was ready to start clearing the rubble of my past and building something new. The work of recovery is never done, but with each step forward, I was learning to embrace the journey of becoming the man I was meant to be.

CHAPTER 5

CLEARING THE RUBBLE

The wreckage of my past lay scattered around me, a constant reminder of the destruction I had caused. Before I could rebuild my life, I had to face the rubble head-on, acknowledge the damage, and begin the painstaking process of clearing it away. It was a daunting task, one that required me to confront the pain I had inflicted on others and the distorted beliefs that had governed my actions for so long.

One of the most difficult aspects of this process was witnessing the ripple effect of my addiction on those closest to me, particularly my mom and my kids' mom. My self-esteem was so low that I had no idea the effect my addiction had on others. For decades, they lived in a state of constant fear, insecurity, and disappointment, all because of my selfish, thoughtless choices. The weight of their suffering was a heavy burden to bear, but it was a necessary part of my journey towards healing.

CLEARING THE RUBBLE

My relationship with my mom had been reduced to a series of brief, tense encounters. For years, she no longer trusted me in her own home and was reduced to handing me plates of food out the back door, silently praying that I would leave quickly. The shame of fully realizing that the intimacy we once shared had been shattered and replaced by a wall of pain and mistrust was a heavy weight to carry. It broke my heart to see how much I had hurt her, but I knew that the only way forward was through honesty and amends.

My kids' mom, the woman who had stood by me through thick and thin, had become a hostage in her own home. She retreated into workaholism, using her career as a shield against the chaos I brought into our lives. I had robbed her of the joy and security she deserved, leaving her to raise our children, Chrissy and Christopher, without a reliable father figure. The guilt I felt was immeasurable, but I knew that guilt without action would not repair the damage.

When the time came to make my amends, I had to sit with the pain I had caused and absorb the impact of my actions. It was a humbling experience, one that required me to listen without argument, defense, or excuses. I had to own my destruction and take responsibility for the years of heartache and disappointment I had inflicted on those I loved most.

Some amends were not made through words alone but through a commitment to living differently. I had to show up as a new man, a better father, son, and partner. This meant being responsible, considerate, honest, and present—qualities I had rarely exhibited in the past. It was a daily practice, a conscious effort to clear the rubble of my past by embodying the principles I was learning in recovery. I had to do what I said and say what I did.

Internally, I had to confront the beliefs and thought patterns that had led me astray. For years, I had operated under the assumption that the world owed me something and that I could cut corners and cheat the system without consequence. My ego and self-will had been my guiding forces, leading me down a path of destruction and despair.

Through the guidance of my sponsors, I began to understand that I was not the center of the universe. In fact, I controlled very little in life. If I wanted to find true peace, I had to learn to submit my will to the care of a higher power and accept that my way of doing things had only brought me pain and suffering.

Clearing the rubble meant deflating my ego, asking for help, and being accountable for my actions. It meant admitting that I was flawed but still worthy of love and redemption. It was a process of surrendering, of letting go of the false pride that had kept me trapped in a cycle of addiction and self-destruction.

CLEARING THE RUBBLE

As I worked through the steps, the shame and baggage of my past began to lighten. I still had to face the consequences of my actions, but I was no longer chained to the guilt and regret that had once consumed me. I started to see my addiction as a tornado that had ripped through my life, leaving behind a trail of rubble that needed to be cleaned up. But I had gotten the tools, the support, and the spiritual foundation to begin the process of rebuilding.

Clearing the rubble was a slow and painstaking process that required patience, perseverance, and a willingness to feel the pain I had avoided for so long. I had to grieve the losses, both material and emotional, that my addiction had caused. I had to rebuild relationships from the ground up, earning back the trust and respect I had squandered. There was no fast-forward button, no shortcut to cleaning up my side of the street.

Some relationships couldn't be salvaged, no matter how much I wished they could. Some people weren't ready to forgive me, and I had to accept that. Just as I had been shown grace and mercy in my own journey, I had to extend that same understanding to others, acknowledging that they were on their own path and that I could not control their feelings or reactions.

In the end, clearing the rubble was about suiting up, showing up, and doing the next right thing. It was about taking responsibility for my life, my choices, and my recovery. One brick at a time, one day at a time, I worked to clean the house, remove the debris of my past, and create a solid foundation for my future.

As I surveyed the landscape of my life, I could see the progress I had made. The rubble was slowly being cleared away, and the wounds were beginning to heal slowly. I knew that there was still work to be done and that the process of rebuilding would be ongoing, but I had faith that with the help of my higher power, my sponsors, and the fellowship of recovery, I could lay a new foundation—one built on honesty, integrity, and service to others. The journey ahead was uncertain, but I was ready to face it, one step at a time.

And so, with the rubble of my past slowly clearing, I turned my attention to the future, to the task of laying a new foundation upon which to build a life of purpose, passion, and peace. The tools were in my hands, the support was by my side, and the path was lit before me. It was time to start building.

CHAPTER 6

LAYING A NEW FOUNDATION

Laying a new foundation for my life meant embracing the principles of recovery, cultivating a genuine relationship with God, and dedicating myself to serving others. The 12 steps aren't for everyone, but they are for me. They became the bedrock of this new foundation, guiding me. While this is my journey, everyone has their own personal expedition. The 12 steps are just tools to use as a touchstone to help dig into the deep work needed for healing.

Steps 1 through 3 focused on repairing my relationship with a higher power. I had to admit my powerlessness over addiction and surrender my will to a force greater than myself. This required a leap of faith and a willingness to believe in something beyond my own understanding. As I worked through these initial steps, I began to experience a glimmer of hope, a sense that perhaps there was a way out of the darkness that had consumed me for so long.

Steps 4 through 9 were about developing a new relationship with myself. I had to take a fearless moral inventory, confronting the wreckage of my past and the character defects that had driven me to addiction. It was a painful process, but one that was necessary for true healing to occur. As I shared my inventory with my sponsor and made amends to those I had harmed, I felt a weight lifting from my shoulders. I was no longer bound by the secrets and shame that had haunted me for years.

Steps 10 through 12 taught me how to relate to others in a healthy, authentic way. I learned to take a daily inventory of my thoughts and actions, promptly admitting I was wrong and making amends when necessary. I sought to improve my conscious contact with God through prayer and meditation, seeking guidance and strength for each new day. I carried the message of recovery to other addicts, sharing my experience, strength, and hope with those who were still suffering.

My sponsors emphasized that change required more than simply going through the motions. I had to become a seeker of wisdom, immersing myself in the principles of recovery through prayer, meditation, meetings, reading, and studying. It wasn't enough to just talk the talk; I had to walk the walk, living these principles in all my affairs.

LAYING A NEW FOUNDATION

Building real faith in a higher power was a critical component of my new foundation. I learned to start each day on my knees, asking to be relieved of self-will to be of maximum service to God and others. I wrote out a daily gratitude list, acknowledging the blessings in my life and cultivating a sense of appreciation for the gift of sobriety. I practiced turning my will and my life over to the care of God in all matters, big and small. Slowly but surely, my conception of God evolved from a distant, wish-granting entity in the sky to an inner voice guiding me toward a life of purpose and meaning.

Relying on God and the steps provided me with a design for living—a blueprint for navigating the challenges of daily life. The old foundation of my existence had been built on ego, fear, resentment, pride, and self-pity—all the things that had led me to addiction and incarceration. But now, I was constructing a new foundation based on spiritual principles, selfless service, rigorous self-examination, and a deep connection with a higher power. This created a framework for living in reality, dealing with adversity, and being a giver instead of a taker.

I learned to humbly put service and sobriety at the center of my life. This meant making coffee commitments, sponsoring others, taking meetings in jails and prisons, serving as a sober house manager, and always extending a hand to struggling newcomers. It wasn't always convenient or comfortable; there were times when I had to show up and be present, even when I felt restless, irritable, and discontent. But each act of service strengthened my foundation, reinforcing the principles that had saved my life. It takes practice. Like a muscle that can atrophy when you don't go to the gym, recovery needs constant practice and attention.

Laying this new foundation was about internalizing the idea that "to keep it, you gotta give it away." Or "You gotta use it or lose it." The more I poured into others and gave of myself, the more grounded and centered I felt in my own recovery. It was a paradox, but one that proved true time and time again. By focusing on helping others, I was actually helping myself, building a life of purpose and meaning one day at a time.

This new way of living took time and practice. I had to be willing to write inventories, admit when I was wrong, make amends, forgive those who had harmed me, ask for help when I needed it, and trust the process even when I couldn't see immediate results. It was a journey of progress, not perfection, and I had to be patient with myself as I learned and grew.

As I laid this new groundwork of faith and altruism, my whole life began to transform in ways I never could have imagined. I reconnected with my family, mending the relationships that had been shattered by my addiction.

Through friendships with others in recovery, I started a business using the principles of recovery to guide me in my professional life. And I developed a deep sense of compassion for others, recognizing that we are all fighting our own battles and deserving of love and support.

Sobriety gave me a second chance at getting it right, and the recovery process laid the foundation for everything that came after—a new way of life. As I focused on service and surrendered my will to a higher power, God put opportunities and people in my path to help me rebuild. All I had to do was suit up, show up, and do the footwork. The results were in His hands.

Looking back, I can see how each step of the journey, each act of service, and each moment of surrender was like laying a brick in the foundation of my new life. It was a slow, sometimes painful process, but one that was essential for long-term recovery and spiritual growth. And as I continued to build on that foundation, brick by brick, day by day, I discovered a sense of purpose and fulfillment that I had never known before.

Laying a new foundation was just the beginning. With a solid base in place, I was ready to start building something beautiful—something that could withstand the storms of life and provide shelter for others who were still struggling. I had no idea what the future held, but I knew that as long as I stayed committed to the principles of recovery and the service of others, I would always have a firm footing on which to stand.

My recovery journey taught me that I was no longer a victim of my circumstances but a builder of my own destiny. With that realization, I was ready to embrace my role as a creator, a shaper of my own life and the lives of those around me. The foundation was laid; it was time to start building.

CHAPTER 7

BECOMING A BUILDER

With solid ground under my feet, I could start constructing a new life aligned with spiritual principles. I became a builder in every sense—creating a recovery community, restoring my family, and building a business.

My friend Anthony, the owner of It's About Change, saw something in me that I hadn't yet seen in myself. He offered me the opportunity to transition from a resident to a manager, running the first sober living home for men I had joined. It was a chance to put my newfound principles into practice and help others find the same solid ground I had discovered.

As a house manager, my responsibilities extended far beyond keeping the place clean and orderly. I was tasked with creating an atmosphere of recovery, a space where men could heal, grow, and prepare to re-enter the world. I enforced the rules, led meetings, and guided residents through the challenges of early sobriety.

Most importantly, I had to model the behavior I wanted to see. I couldn't just talk the talk; I had to walk the walk.

Together, Anthony and I built a strong recovery community. We organized speaker events, group outings, and service commitments. We cultivated an ethos of tough love, balancing compassion with accountability. I learned that sometimes the most loving thing you can do for an addict is to hold them accountable for refusing to enable their destructive behaviors. It wasn't always easy, but it was vital.

Helping other men gave me a sense of purpose, a reason to get out of bed in the morning. It kept me out of my own head, away from the self-centered thinking that had dominated my life for so long. Even on the days when I was struggling and the weight of my past threatened to pull me back down, I had to show up as a leader. I had to be the man these guys needed me to be.

Being of service became the cornerstone of my new life. It also helped heal my own broken relationships. My father, stepfather, and grandfather were all men who contributed to wounds in my life. This was a way I could create a new narrative and reconstruct positive relationships with other men, and it was a gift.

Outside the recovery house, I started the slow process of rebuilding my relationships with my children, Chrissy and Christopher, and their mother. I had to construct a new identity as

BECOMING A BUILDER

a father and co-parent, one built on consistency, reliability, and love.

I committed to being present in their lives, to showing up for birthdays, holidays, school events, and sports games. I called them regularly, not just to check a box but to genuinely connect. I offered my time, not just my money. I had missed so much, and I knew I could never get that time back, but I could make the most of the time I had now.

My kids were understandably skeptical at first. They had heard promises before, only to be disappointed time and time again. They had wounds that needed to be healed, and I couldn't blame them for their hesitancy. I accepted it. I had to demonstrate that I was trustworthy through my changed behavior over time. Slowly, day by day, I rebuilt the bond with my children. They began to let me back into their hearts, and I cherished every moment of that hard-won trust.

With their mother, I had to establish healthy boundaries and communication. We weren't romantically involved anymore, but we were still a team when it came to raising our children. She had always seen my potential, even when I couldn't see it myself. She had long waited for me to be the man she knew I could be. It wasn't easy, but we learned to co-parent with respect, putting our kids' needs first.

My mom was one of the last relationships I restored. I had put her through so much, and the shame of my actions kept me from reaching out at first. I had to humble myself to let her see that my life was truly different now. I included her in my recovery, inviting her to meetings and celebrations. I made living amends by being a better son and showing up for her in ways I hadn't before. Slowly, her trust in me was restored, and our relationship blossomed in ways I could never have imagined.

Professionally, I reunited with old recovery friends, Jason and Mike, to start a pest control business that would come to flourish. I used my newfound leadership skills to build and train teams, implement systems, and scale the company. My recovery principles translated seamlessly into the business world. I focused on hiring good people, being of service to customers, working with integrity, and giving back to the community.

As the business grew, I learned that success isn't just about revenue; it's about building something of value, something that makes a difference in people's lives. The more I focused on lifting up the people around me—my employees, customers, and community—the more abundance flowed into my life. It was a lesson in the power of service—the very same lesson I had learned in recovery.

Becoming a builder meant developing a new identity, one rooted in integrity, consistency, and service. It wasn't a one-time event but a daily practice. I had to construct that identity through the work of recovery, through the small choices and actions that added up over time. As I built up the recovery community, my family relationships, and the business, I realized something else was being built: a new me.

I was becoming the man I had always wanted to be, the man I was meant to be. It wasn't easy, and it wasn't perfect, but it was progress. And for the first time in my life, I was proud of the man I saw in the mirror.

The transformation happening within me was tapped into something much larger than myself. The true essence of strength is found in the inner realms of the spirit of intention. Yet, as I soon discovered, this isn't the kind of strength our world typically recognizes or understands. What does embracing true strength require of us?

CHAPTER 8

EMBRACING TRUE STRENGTH

The women in my life are nothing short of awe-inspiring. The longer I live, the more I understand how special they are. Throughout my journey of personal transformation, I've come to understand the profound impact they've had on my life and how they contributed to shaping the man I am today.

Their unwavering strength, resilience, and capacity to love in the face of adversity have been a guiding light, illuminating the path to my own growth and healing. From my mother to my daughter's mother to my aunts, these remarkable women have taught me invaluable lessons about the true nature of strength.

Growing up, I witnessed my mother endure unimaginable hardships. She faced abuse, poverty, and abandonment, yet somehow managed to create a loving home for my brother and me. I can still remember the nights when she would come home late, her face stained with tears from fighting for her life. Even in

EMBRACING THE TRUE STRENGTH

those moments of despair, she never let go of her determination to provide for us.

There were times when my mother couldn't even afford to put food on the table, but she never let that break her spirit. I watched in awe as she took a minimum-wage job at a currency exchange, working tirelessly to make ends meet. Her resilience in the face of adversity was a testament to the quiet, steadfast strength that burned within her.

When my mother found God, her faith became an unshakable force that transformed her life. She quit smoking and ended toxic relationships with men cold turkey. It was inspiring. Her prayers became a lifeline for me, even when I was at my lowest point and didn't want to live. I could feel the power of her love and faith, holding me up when I couldn't stand on my own.

My kids' mother, too, showed a wise and powerful kind of strength. Despite the chaos and pain I brought into our lives through my addiction, she never let it tarnish the love our children had for me. I put her through hell, yet she demonstrated an extraordinary capacity for endurance and enablement. She tolerated manipulation and theft that would have shattered most relationships, yet somehow she found the strength to keep going. Her loyalty was a testament to the depth of her love and the resilience of her spirit. Every Christmas, she made sure my name was on the gifts, creating the illusion that I was present even when

I wasn't. She never spoke ill of me. She could have easily turned our kids against me, and no one would have blamed her, but she chose to protect the bond we shared.

I'll never forget the day I spoke to my daughter on a phone call from jail. She was only nine years old and distraught and confused because she had just started her period. At that moment, from behind the bars of my jail cell, I was the only person she felt she could talk to. We shared a bond that transcended the distance between us, and I listened and consoled her as best I could. It broke my heart not to be there with her in person, to hold her hand, and to be present like a dad should be. I needed to get through to her that what was happening was normal and natural, unlike how the only way to talk to her dad was to reach him in jail. I was grateful that she trusted me enough to confide in me, but I also felt like a failure as a father, unable to give her my all like I desperately wanted.

My aunts, too, were a force to be reckoned with. What they lacked in refinement, they made up for in sheer determination. They had a way of making things happen, whether it was acquiring nice things or navigating complex family dynamics. Their sense of entitlement both helped and hindered them, but I couldn't help but admire their tenacity.

As I began sponsoring men in recovery, I quickly realized that I had a blind spot when it came to understanding the experience of the addict's mother. Watching these women shoulder the burdens of their families while their loved ones spiraled out of control was a humbling experience. I saw my own selfishness reflected back at me, and I began to understand how I had exploited the strength of the women who loved me. I had weaponized their tolerance and abused their ability to bounce back from the pain I inflicted.

Making amends with the women I had harmed was one of the most challenging and humbling experiences of my recovery. I had to confront the ways in which I had taken their strength for granted, adding to their already heavy load with my own weakness. I realized that I could never truly repay the debt I owed them, but I could commit to being a steady, positive presence in their lives moving forward.

Through this process, I learned that real strength isn't about being loud or dominating. It's not about hiding behind a facade or pretending your fear is anger. It's the ability to bear impossible burdens, bounce back from crushing disappointment, and see the best in people even when they show you their worst. Women seem to possess this strength naturally, and I am in awe of their resilience.

Today, I strive to honor the strength of the women who have held me up by being a rock for the people in my life. When I feel exhausted or overwhelmed, I think of how these women never stopped fighting for me, even when I gave them every reason to give up. Their example propels me to keep going and to be the man they always believed I could be.

Embracing the true strength of the women in my life has been a transformative experience, one that has taught me the power of resilience, faith, and unconditional love. As I continue on my journey of recovery and growth, I carry their lessons with me, determined to channel my own strength in the service of others.

In my quest for inner peace and purpose, I've come to understand that trusting in a power greater than myself is essential. But learning to have faith in the unseen is easier said than done, especially for someone like me who has always relied on my own wits and will to survive.

CHAPTER 9

TRUSTING THE UNSEEN

Faith is a funny thing. It's not tangible, not something you can hold in your hands or point to and say, "There it is." But as I've journeyed through recovery, I've come to understand that faith is key and the bedrock upon which my new life is built. It's the quiet assurance that even when I can't see the path ahead, even when the future seems uncertain or downright scary, I can trust an unseen power at work, guiding me, shaping me, and preparing me for something greater than I could ever imagine. I feel it in my soul.

In the early days of my recovery, faith almost seemed like a joke to me. In my bitter heart and closed mind, it felt like a foreign concept. I was so used to relying on myself—on my own wits and my own strength—that the idea of surrendering to a higher power seemed ludicrous. I remember sitting in meetings, listening to people talk about God, and rolling my eyes.

"What a bunch of crap."

But deep down, I yearned for a substance that wasn't something you could shoot or smoke. I needed purpose and something more than myself to get through this. So, I started with the basics. I leaned on mantras like "fake it till you make it" and "act as if." I didn't really believe it, but I hoped that if I just kept going through the motions, eventually it would click. My sponsor, Mahat, was instrumental in helping me understand what true faith looks like. He taught me that faith isn't just about believing in something unseen; it's about taking action, even when you can't see the results.

"Faith is facing your fear and doing it anyway," he would say. "It's finishing the steps, even when you don't understand how they're going to help you. It's being of service, even when you don't feel like it. It's submitting your will, even when every fiber of your being wants to resist."

At first, none of it made sense to me. I couldn't see how working the steps or helping others was going to magically fix my life. But Mahat insisted that I keep doing it anyway.

"Trust the process," he would say. "Keep putting one foot in front of the other, and eventually, you'll look back and see how far you've come."

So that's what I did. I white-knuckled my addiction for 10 years before I understood the beauty of recovery. I was sober, but I was not living the life of recovery until I truly surrendered.

TRUSTING THE UNSEEN

I started looking for God's fingerprints in my life, even in the smallest of ways. I saw it in the compassionate intake officer who went out of her way to get me into treatment, even though I didn't deserve it. I saw it in my mom's tough love when she closed the door in my face on that record-cold, freezing night, knowing that sometimes the most loving thing you can do is let someone hit their bottom. I saw it in action—the way my life started to come together, piece by piece, as I cleared away the wreckage of my past and laid a new foundation based on honesty, integrity, and service.

As I continued to work on my recovery, I began to see that even my darkest moments had been preparing me for my brightest future. Every hurt, every rejection, every failure was composting my character, turning the shit of my past into fertilizer for my growth. I had to reframe my painful childhood not as a tragedy but as the perfect training ground for empathy and survival. I saw God's hand in putting mentors like Anthony, Steve, and Rob in my path—men who could father my development in ways my own father never could.

In business, too, I had to learn to trust the process. Building a company is not an overnight endeavor; it's a brick-by-brick journey that requires patience, persistence, and faith. At Platinum Pest Solutions, we poured into our people, trusting that if we created a culture of growth and service, the right revenue and results would follow. When challenges arose, as they inevitably do, I had to resist the urge to control everything and instead pray for guidance and surrender to the outcome.

With my family, I had to accept that I couldn't repair all the damage I'd done overnight. I had to keep showing up, keep doing the next right thing, and trust that God would restore us in His own time. I let go of my timeline and my expectations, focusing instead on being the best father, son, and brother I could be, one day at a time.

Perhaps the most profound lesson in trusting the unseen has come through my experience as a sponsor. Walking alongside others in their recovery journey, I've had to accept that I'm not in control of anyone's sobriety but my own. My job is to show them how I'm living, to share my experience, strength, and hope, and to detach with love. That's it. Their personal accountability and higher power are in charge of the outcome.

Over and over, I've seen that when I give my best where I am with what I have, the results are better than I could have planned. I've learned to set intentions instead of expectations, to show up fully in each moment, and to trust God to sort out the details. The more I let go of my ideas about how it's supposed to go, the more ease and abundance I feel. I've realized I don't have to white-knuckle my will; I can relax into the current of grace.

One of the greatest gifts of recovery has been developing faith in the unseen. I trust that no matter what life throws at me, I can turn it over, suit up, show up, and let God handle the rest. This doesn't mean I get to kick back and coast. Trusting the unseen means I have to keep doing the footwork and spiritual maintenance daily. I embrace routines and do daily meditations. But I can release the results and embrace the journey with peace.

As I reflect on my journey, I'm filled with gratitude for the beautiful mystery of faith. It has carried me through the darkest of times and led me to a life beyond my wildest dreams. And though I may not always understand the plan, I know deep in my soul that I am exactly where I'm meant to be, guided by a loving power greater than myself. The light of this truth illuminates my path, casting out the shadows of doubt and fear and showing me the way forward, one step at a time.

CHAPTER 10

LIVING IN THE LIGHT

The journey from darkness to light is a path that I once thought was impossible. For years, I was trapped in the quicksand of addiction, sinking deeper with each passing day. The more I struggled and fought against it in my own mind, the more I found myself consumed by the weight of my own demons. But today, I stand as an active testament to the transformative power of recovery. I am living proof that, through willingness and spiritual principles, even the most lost among us can find their way back to the light.

My recovery is not a destination, but rather a work in progress. My vision is to evolve and become a better man every day. Recovery is not static; it is active work, but it is also a gift that must be protected. Like a living thing, it is something to be nourished in order to healthfully thrive. The key to maintaining this precious gift lies in the simple yet profound act of helping others while honoring your own authenticity. Through sponsorship, I have the privilege of guiding men through the same work that changed my life. I challenge them to dig deep, confront their darkest truths, and emerge on the other side with a newfound sense of honesty, integrity, and purpose.

The process is simple, but not easy. It is also essential. I ask them to take uncomfortable actions, step outside of their comfort zones, and put their faith in a higher power. For some, this means finding a God of their understanding. For others, it means surrendering to the collective wisdom of the fellowship. Regardless of the path they choose, the goal remains the same: to break free from the chains of addiction and to live a life of freedom and peace.

In my professional life, I have the unique opportunity to bring the principles of recovery into the workplace. As a coach and mentor to our managers, I encourage them to practice acceptance, accountability, and character-building. We work together to create a culture of integrity where a moral compass guides every decision. The results have been nothing short of remarkable. By putting recovery at the center of our business, we have not only strengthened our bottom line but also created a community of individuals who are committed to personal and professional growth.

My role as a father is perhaps the most important one I will ever play. I strive to be a steady presence of love and wisdom for my children, even when it means challenging them to step outside of their comfort zones. I know that my words and actions have the power to shape their lives, and I take that responsibility seriously. It's not always easy, and I'm not always the most popular parent when I push them to grow, but I know in my heart that it's the most valuable gift I can give them.

Throughout my journey, I have been blessed with an incredible support system. Anthony, Rob, and my core circle of recovery mentors have been by my side through the darkest times. They knew me and believed in me when I was at my lowest, and they never gave up on me. They continue to hold me accountable, call me out when I'm not living up to my potential, and remind me that I'm not in control. Their guidance and wisdom keep me grounded, reminding me that to keep growing, I must stay on the right track and remember that I'm not the one driving this bus.

My personal ambitions have shifted dramatically since I first stepped into the rooms of recovery. I no longer chase the fleeting highs of material success or external validation. Instead, my ultimate goal is to find serenity and live a life of altruism. I want to be a beacon of hope for those who are still struggling, to show them that change is possible, no matter how far gone they may feel. I know firsthand the depths of despair that addiction can bring, and I feel a deep sense of responsibility to share the message of recovery with anyone who wants it.

LIVING IN THE LIGHT

But living in the light is not a one-time event. It is a daily practice that requires vigilance, humility, and a willingness to confront the darkness when it inevitably creeps back in. I have to be mindful of my motives, clean up any resentments that may be festering beneath the surface, and be willing to admit when I'm wrong. The ego is a cunning and baffling adversary, always waiting for an opportunity to reassert its dominance. It's like a weed that must be constantly tended to lest it overtake the garden of the soul.

I remember the first time I spoke at a recovery convention. As I looked out at the sea of faces before me, I saw a reflection of myself from 20 years earlier. I saw the pain, the confusion, and the desperation that come with active addiction. But I also saw a glimmer of hope and a flicker of light in their eyes, which told me they were ready for change. At that moment, I knew that my purpose was to illuminate the path that had been lit for me, to show them that there was a way out of the darkness.

To anyone who is still suffering, I want to offer a message of hope. There is a solution, and it is within your reach. It won't be easy, and it will require a level of commitment and vulnerability that may seem impossible at first. But I promise you, it is worth it. The 12 steps offer a blueprint for transformation, a roadmap to a life beyond your wildest dreams. All you have to do is take that first step and admit that you are powerless over your addiction and that your life has become unmanageable. It may not be a 12-

step program that works for you, but if you follow the principles, you will find your own personal journey for change.

From there, the journey of recovery will unfold before you. You will learn to lean on a power greater than yourself, to take a fearless moral inventory, and to make amends for the wrongs you have done. You will discover a fellowship of individuals who understand your personal struggle and who will walk beside you every step of the way. There are no big shots in recovery; there is only a community of equals who are all working towards the same goal: to live a life of purpose, integrity, and joy.

The path of recovery is not a straight line. There will be twists and turns, ups and downs, moments of triumph, and moments of despair. But through it all, the principles of the program will guide you. You will learn to take contrary action when your instincts tell you to retreat, to reach out when you want to isolate, and to keep going when you want to quit. The miracle of recovery is that it works if you work it. Yes, this is 12 Step Talk, but it's true.

My greatest teachers in this life have been my pain and the 12 steps. Pain was the catalyst that finally made me willing to try a new way of life and admit that I couldn't do it on my own. The steps provided me with a framework for transformation—a set of principles that I could apply to every aspect of my existence. I had to be broken down to my very foundation in order to break through to the other side.

Looking back, I can see that every experience, every trial and tribulation, was perfectly orchestrated to bring me to this moment. I don't regret a single second of my journey because it is what it is. It's reality, which is so much more fulfilling than delusion or escapism. Without it, I wouldn't have found the healing and satisfaction that come with embracing recovery. I have developed a relationship with a higher power, myself, and the world around me that fills me with an overwhelming sense of gratitude and purpose.

So, to anyone who is reading these words, I want to leave you with a simple message: no matter how lost you may feel, no matter how deep the darkness may seem, there is always hope. Always. You can emerge from the quicksand of addiction and live a life beyond your wildest dreams. All it takes is a willingness to try, a humble heart, and an unrelenting desire to grow along spiritual lines.

If a hopeless addict like me can find a way out, then so can you. The light is nonjudgmental, and there is a whole community of people ready to walk beside you on your journey. All you have to do is take that first step, reach out your hand, and ask for help. From there, the miracle of recovery will unfold, and you will discover a world of grace, peace, and purpose you never knew existed.

Let's walk this path together, one day at a time. Let's share our experience, strength, and hope with each other, and let's create a ripple effect of healing that touches every corner of the earth. Because, in the end, that's what recovery is all about—living in the light by living authentically and doing the work. This is what brings meaning to our lives and offers hope to all who are still trapped in the darkness.